THE MOTHER GOOSE SONGBOOK

BY TOM GLAZER

ILLUSTRATED BY
DAVID McPHAIL

DOUBLEDAY

NEW YORK · LONDON · TORONTO · SYDNEY · AUCKLAND

For Lisa Ariel and Rebecca Margaret Glazer
—T.G.

For Ebony
(JILL, PAGE 25)
and for all her classmates and teachers
at The Wentworth School,
Portsmouth, New Hampshire
—D.M.

Published by Doubleday,
a division of
Bantam Doubleday Dell Publishing Group, Inc.
666 Fifth Avenue, New York, New York 10103

Doubleday
and the portrayal of an anchor with a dolphin
are trademarks of Doubleday, a division of
Bantam Doubleday Dell Publishing Group, Inc.

Library of Congress Cataloging-in-Publication Data
The Mother Goose songbook.
Summary: An illustrated collection of traditional
nursery rhymes set to music.
1. Children's songs.   2. Nursery rhymes—Musical
settings. [1. Nursery rhymes.   2. Songs.] I. Glazer,
Tom.   II. McPhail, David M., ill.   III. Mother Goose.
M1997.M9186   1990   88-753151
ISBN 0-385-41474-9
ISBN 0-385-24631-5 (pbk.)

Designed by: Diane Stevenson/SNAP • HAUS GRAPHICS

Piano arrangements, original words and music
and adaptations of traditional words and music
Copyright © 1990 by Tom Glazer, Songs Music, Inc.,
Scarborough, N.Y. 10510

Illustrations copyright © 1990 by David McPhail

CONTENTS

Who Was Mother Goose?

The earliest known printed reference to a Mother Goose appeared in France in 1697, in a collection of fairy tales called *Contes de Ma Mère L'Oye* (Stories of My Mother Goose), by Charles Perrault. But these were fairy tales, not the verses that have come down to us in English.

Then, in England, almost a century later in 1781, there appeared a book published by John Newbery, entitled *Mother Goose's Melody: or, Sonnets from the Cradle—the Most Celebrated Songs and Lullabies of Old British Nurses.* Newbery's title was probably borrowed from Charles Perrault's earlier volume, but *only* the title. Four years after its appearance in England, an edition was published in the United States in 1785 by Isaiah Thomas.

But before this a legend sprang up here about a New England lady named Elizabeth Goose (or Vergoose, or Vertigoose), who is supposed to be buried in an old Boston graveyard, the Old Granary Burying Ground. Tourists are still attracted to the site. In 1719 she was supposed to have written a book of rhymes for children, which book created the legend, because of her name, that she was the original Mother Goose. But not one copy of her book, if indeed she ever wrote one, has ever surfaced, and so scholars are very dubious about the accuracy of this legend.

And that, more or less, is what we know of the origin of the lady known as Mother Goose.

Political Origins

A few scholars have claimed that at least a few or perhaps more Mother Goose rhymes originated as a sort of political "double-speak," or shorthand code to reflect illegal or unpopular political opinion in England. (See *The Annotated Mother Goose* by W. S. Baring-Gould, 1957.)

For example, we are surprised to be told that the familiar "Taffy Was a Welshman" may have originated with Englishmen who lived on the Welsh border, as a rhyme to poke fun at Welshmen. This they customarily did on St. David's Day in Wales, the first of March, St. David being the patron saint of the Welsh and "Taffy" being a variant of "Davy."

Again we learn that, according to the scholar Katherine Elwes Thomas, "Baa, Baa, Black Sheep" is actually a verse which expresses a complaint by the common folks of England (the "little boy who lives in the lane" is supposed to symbolize the common people) against the King ("one for my master") and against the rich nobility ("one for my Dame"); the ruler and his nobles were taking too large a portion of the wool made by sheep farmers.

All of this may or may not be true; no one seems to know for certain. What is important, however, is that lovers of Mother Goose—children, parents, and teachers—see no controversy; they unequivocally adore Mother Goose, whoever or whatever she is. For hundreds of years in the past, on into the present, and into the foreseeable and unforeseeable future, we will continue to cherish these simple, charming, touching, and often beautiful rhymes. The British poet Walter de la Mare puts it this way: "Mother Goose rhymes fill the fancy, charm tongue and ear, delight the inner eye, and many of them are tiny masterpieces of word craftsmanship. . ."

Mother Goose herself is traditionally depicted as an old woman with a hooked nose and a long chin, riding on a flying gander. This is interesting and rather puzzling, for such a facial description is usually that of a witch. I don't know why beloved Mother Goose has been illustrated this way, but perhaps it is possible to have a hooked nose and a long chin and be a benign person, or to have a sharp chin and a long nose and be a haglike witch.

There are many, many Mother Goose books; possibly hundreds have appeared through the years. Why another one? Because we think that this one differs in one important way: all the rhymes are set to music, a situation not commonly found. Across the centuries many of the famous rhymes have, of course, been set to music. Some of these melodies have become popular and have lasted; others have not and have died out or lie buried in forgotten books. And some of the rhymes seem never to be sung. I grew up learning several wonderful tunes to Mother Goose rhymes and wondered why other rhymes had no tunes.

It occurred to me, then, to collect those rhymes with excellent melodies and to add original tunes to other rhymes in order to present a collection of Mother Goose in which all the rhymes therein could be sung and played and not merely recited. But I dared also to do something further, something I had not previously planned on, something which came to me as I was putting down the words and music: to add, occasionally, an additional verse to some of the existing verses, the traditional ones. I hope the reader, be he or she ever so traditionalist, will not mind too much. And I hope these words and the new melodies have kept the Mother Goose tradition intact. In any case, Mother Goose, bless her, is still alive and well, and we are most fortunate that such an endearing creature, in a too ephemeral world, remains immortal.

THE
MOTHER GOOSE
SONGBOOK

Baa, Baa, Black Sheep

1. Baa, baa, black sheep, have you an - y wool?
2. Baa, baa, black sheep, will you crop my lawn?

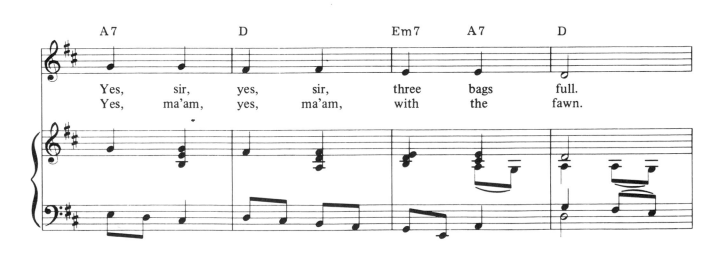

Yes, sir, yes, sir, three bags full.
Yes, ma'am, yes, sir, ma'am, three with the fawn.

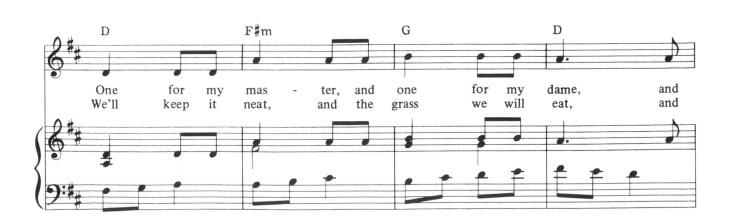

One for my mas - ter, and one for my dame, and
We'll keep it neat, and the grass we will eat, and

one   for the lit - tle boy who lives   in the   lane.
I'll   play the sum - mer day and bleat,   bleat, ___ bleat.

THE FARMER IN THE DELL

1. The farm - er in the dell, the farm - er in the dell. Heigh - o the der - ry - o, the farm - er in the dell.

2. The farm - er takes a wife, the farm - er takes a wife, Heigh - o the der - ry - o, the farm - er takes a wife.

3. The wife takes a nurse, *etc.*

4. The nurse takes a child . . .

5. The child takes a dog . . .

6. The dog takes a cat . . .

7. The cat takes a rat . . .

8. The rat takes the cheese . . .

9. The cheese stands alone . . .

GOOSEY, GOOSEY GANDER

Slowly

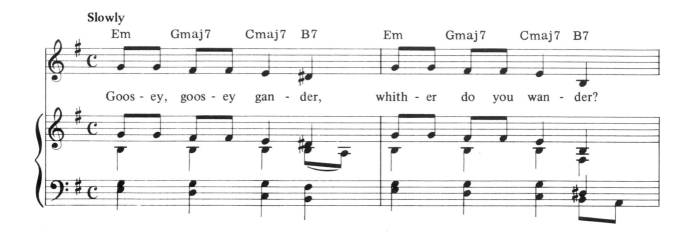

Goos - ey, goos - ey gan - der, whith - er do you wan - der?

Up - stairs and down - stairs, and in my la - dy's cham - ber.

There I met an old man who would not say his pray'rs; I

HEY DIDDLE DIDDLE

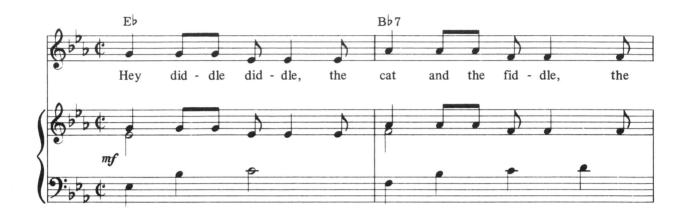

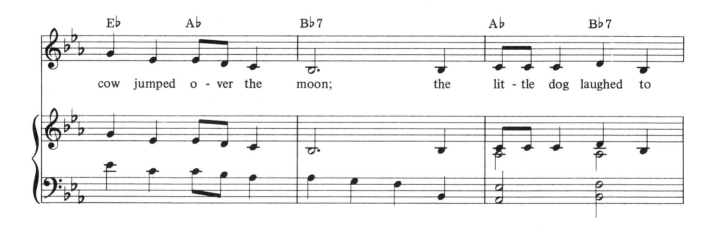

spoon, spoon, spoon, the dish ran a-way with the spoon.

2. Hey diddle diddle, the cat's on the griddle,
   the puppy's chewing the broom;
   a worm's in the batter,
   but it doesn't matter,
   we'll crawl all over the room, room, room,
   we'll crawl all over the room.

HICKORY DICKORY DOCK

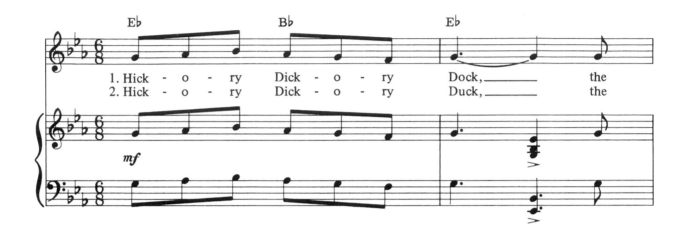

1. Hick - o - ry Dick - o - ry Dock,_____ the
2. Hick - o - ry Dick - o - ry Duck,_____ the

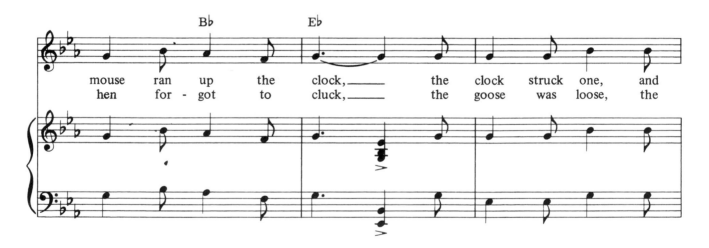

mouse ran up the clock,_____ the clock struck one, and
hen for - got to cluck,_____ the goose was loose, and the

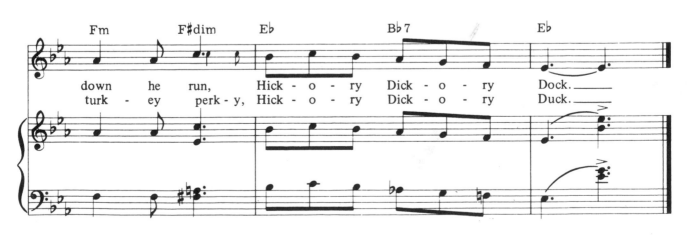

down he run, Hick - o - ry Dick - o - ry Dock._____
turk - ey perk - y, Hick - o - ry Dick - o - ry Duck._____

16

3. Hickory Dickory Deck,
   A frog jumped on my neck,
   The frog said, "Croak,"
   I gave him a poke,
   Hickory Dickory Deck.

HOT CROSS BUNS

19

All the king's hors - es and all the king's men, could - n't
Down came a fair - y who waved her wand then, and she

put Humpt - ty Dump - ty to - geth - er a - gain.
put Humpt - ty Dump - ty to - geth - er a - gain.

I Had a Little Nut Tree

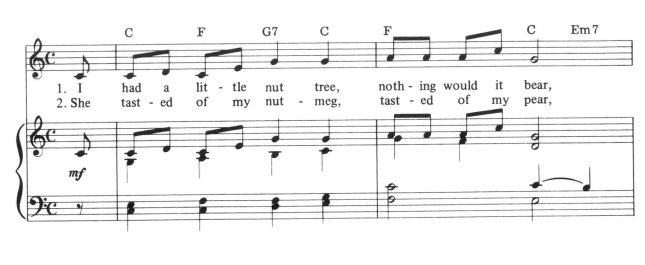

1. I had a little nut tree, noth-ing would it bear,
2. She tast-ed of my nut-meg, tast-ed of my pear,

But a sil-ver nut-meg, and a gold-en pear. The
sat with me and let me bind her gold-en hair. The

King of Spain's daugh-ter came to vis-it me, and
King of Spain's daugh-ter kissed me wild and free, and

JACK AND JILL

1. Jack and Jill went up the hill to
2. up Jack got and Jill home did trot as

fetch a pail of wa - ter,
fast as he could ca - per, To

Jack fell down and broke his crown, and
old Dame Dob who patched his nob with

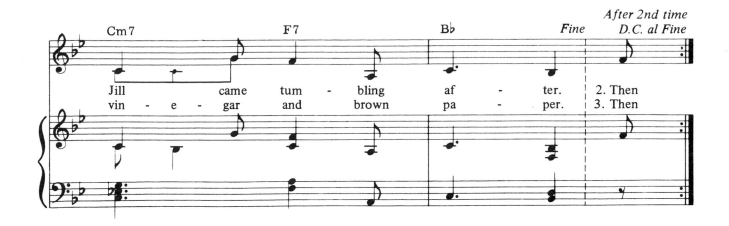

Jill   came tum - bling   af - ter. | 2. Then
vin - e - gar and   brown   pa - per. | 3. Then

3. Then Jill came in, and she did grin
   to see Jack's paper plaster;
   her mother spanked her across her knee
   for laughing at Jack's disaster.

LAZY MARY

1. La - zy Mar - y, will you get up, will you get up, will you get up? La - zy Mar - y, will you get up, so ear - ly in the morn - ing?

2. No, no, moth - er, I won't get up, I won't get up, I won't get up. No, no, moth - er, I won't get up, I won't get up to - day.

27

LITTLE BO PEEP

1. Lit - tle Bo Peep has lost her sheep and
2. Lit - tle Bo Peep fell fast a - sleep and

can't tell where _____ to find them;
dreamt she heard _____ them bleat - ing; but

Leave them a - lone and they'll come home
when she a - woke it was a joke,

28

LITTLE BOY BLUE

Slowly

G   **Am/G**

1. Lit - tle Boy Blue, come blow your horn, the
2. I've of - ten won - dered while go - ing to sleep, if

p   ✳ *simile*

C/G   **D7/G**   **G**

sheep's in the mead - ow, the cow's in **the** corn,
Lit - tle Boy Blue___ knew Lit - tle **Bo** Peep,

G   **Am/G**

Where is the boy who looks af - ter the sheep? He's
Were they good friends as they tend - ed their sheep, and

30

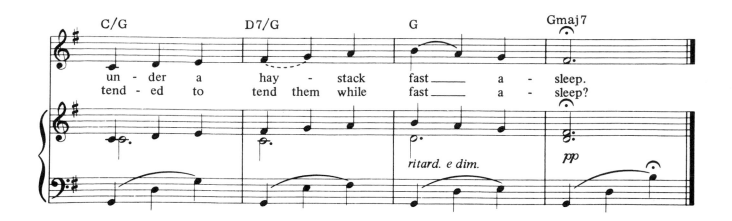

un - der a hay - stack fast _____ a - sleep.
tend - ed to tend them while fast _____ a - sleep?

ritard. e dim. *pp*

LITTLE JACK HORNER

LITTLE MISS MUFFET

LONDON BRIDGE

1. Lon - don Bridge is fall - ing down,
2. Build it up with i - ron bars,

3. Iron bars will bend and break . . .   4. Build it up with silver and gold . . .

LUCY LOCKET

MARY HAD A LITTLE LAMB

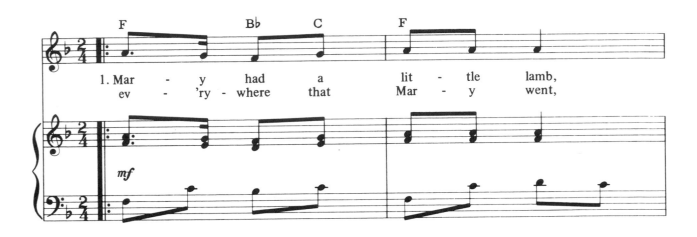

1. Mar - y had a lit - tle lamb,
ev - 'ry - where that Mar - y went,

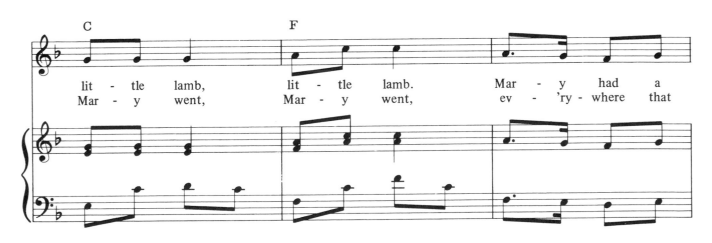

lit - tle lamb, lit - tle lamb. Mar - y had a
Mar - y went, Mar - y went, ev - 'ry - where that

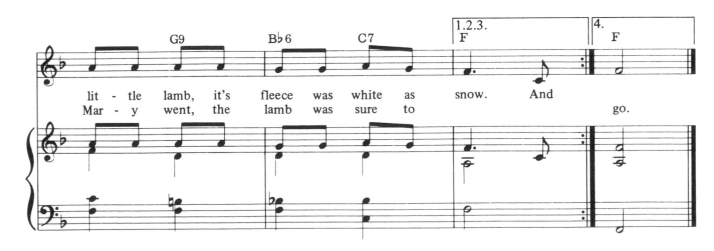

lit - tle lamb, it's fleece was white as snow. And
Mar - y went, the lamb was sure to go.

2. It followed her to school one day, . . . *etc.*
   which was against the rule.
   It made the children laugh and play, . . . *etc.*
   To see a lamb at school.

3. And so the teacher chased it out, . . . *etc.*
   But still it lingered near.
   And waited patiently, ly, ly, . . . *etc.*
   Till Mary did appear.

4. "What makes the lamb love Mary so?", . . . *etc.*
   The eager children cry.
   "Oh Mary loves the lamb, you know," . . . *etc.*
   The teacher did reply.

MISTRESS MARY

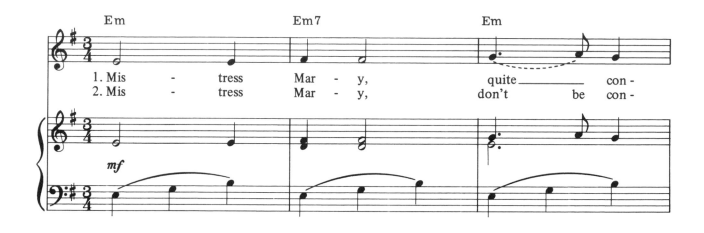

1. Mis - tress Mar - y, quite____ con -
2. Mis - tress Mar - y, don't be con -

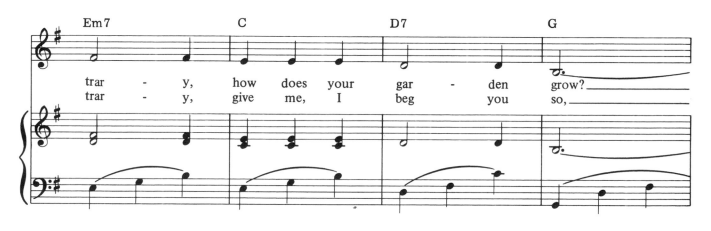

trar - y, how does your gar - den grow?____
trar - y, give me, I beg you so,____

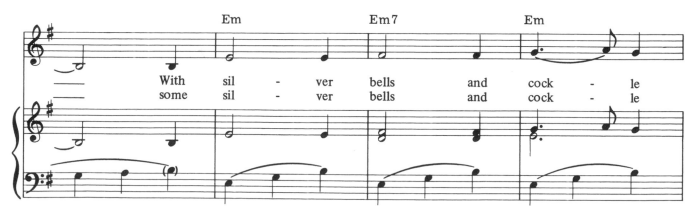

With sil - ver bells and cock - le
some sil - ver bells and cock - le

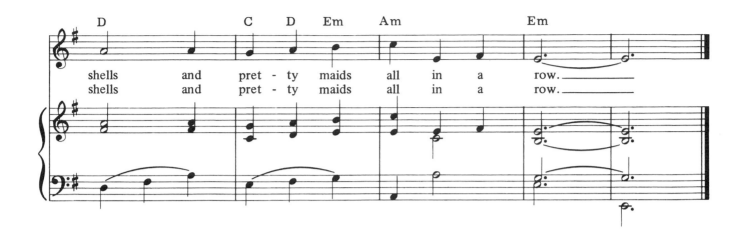

shells and pret - ty maids all in a row. ____

THE MUFFIN MAN

THE MULBERRY BUSH

1. Here we go round the mulberry bush, the mulberry bush, the mulberry bush. Here we go round the mulberry bush, so early in the morning.

2. This is the way we wash our clothes, we wash our clothes, we wash our clothes. This is the way we wash our clothes, so early in the morning.

3. This is the way we iron our clothes, . . . etc.   4. (Repeat Verse 1)

OATS, PEAS, BEANS

OLD KING COLE

Old King Cole was a mer-ry old soul, and a

48

49

ver - y fine fid - dle had he.   Twee - dle

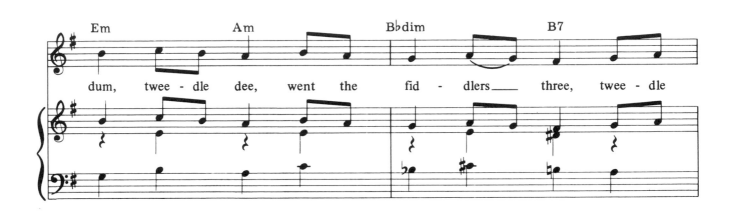

dum, twee - dle dee, went the fid - dlers____ three, twee - dle

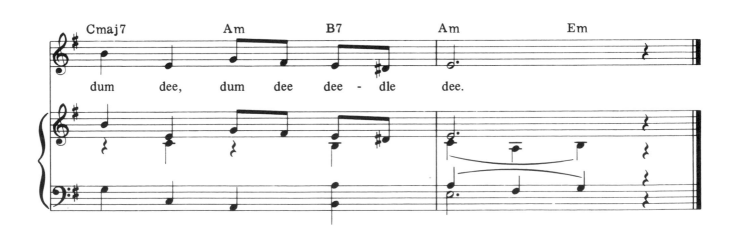

dum dee, dum dee dee - dle dee.

Old MacDonald

moo - moo there,   here a moo, there a moo,   ev - 'ry-where a moo - moo,
oink - oink there,   here an oink, there an oink,   ev - 'ry-where an oink - oink,

Old Mac - Don - ald had a farm, E - I - E - I - O.

(*As above, repeating each animal backward.*)
3. . . . and on his farm he had a duck . . . *etc.*
    with a quack-quack here . . . *etc.*

4. . . . a horse . . .
    with a neigh-neigh here . . . *etc.*

5. . . . a donkey . . .
    with a hee-haw here . . .

6. . . . a hen . . .
    with a cluck-cluck here . . .
(*add other animals*)

OLD MOTHER GOOSE

Old Moth - er Goose, when she want - ed to wan - der, would

ride through the air on a ver - y fine____ gan - der;

Old Fa - ther Gan - der, when the wind was fast and loose, would

OLD MOTHER HUBBARD

1. Old Moth-er Hub-bard went to the cup-board to get her poor dog a bone. But when she got there the cup-board was bare, and so the poor dog had none. She went to the bak-er's to buy him some bread,

55

Dm   Gm   G7   Gm   C7   F   C

when she got home the poor   dog   was dead. She   went   to the un-der-tak-er's to

Bbmaj7   C7   Bb   C7   Bb   F

buy   him a cof-fin,   but when she got   back   the   dog   was   laugh-in'.

(Note: Fit succeeding verses to the tune as best you can.)

2. She took a clean dish to get him some tripe;
   When she came back he was smoking a pipe.
   She went to the alehouse to get him some beer;
   When she came back the dog sat in a chair.
     She went to the tavern for white wine and red;
     When she came back the dog stood on his head.
   She went to the hatter's to buy him a hat;
   When she came back he was feeding the cat.

3. She went to the barber's to buy him a wig;
   When she came back he was dancing a jig.
   She went to the fruit store to buy him some fruit;
   When she came back he was playing the flute.
     She went to the tailor's to buy him a coat;
     When she came back he was riding a goat.
   She went to the cobbler's to buy him some shoes;
   When she came back he was reading the news.

4. She went to the seamster's to buy him some linen;
   When she came back the dog was a-spinning.
   She went to the hosier's to buy him some hose;
   When she came back he was dressed in his clothes.
     The dame made a curtsy; the dog made a bow;
     The dame said, "Your servant;"—the dog said, "Bow-wow."
   Old Mother Hubbard went to the cupboard to get her poor dog a bone.
   But when she got there the cupboard was bare and so the poor dog had none.

Pease Porridge

Pease por - ridge hot, Pease por - ridge cold,

Pease por - ridge in the pot nine days old.

Some like it hot, some like it cold,

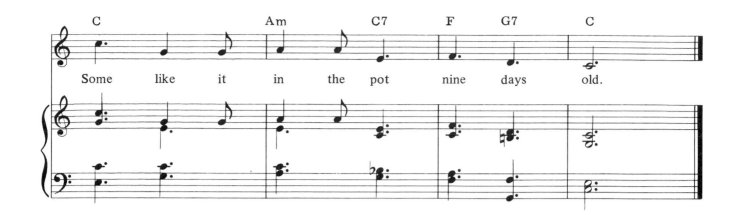

Some like it in the pot nine days old.

PETER, PETER, PUMPKIN EATER

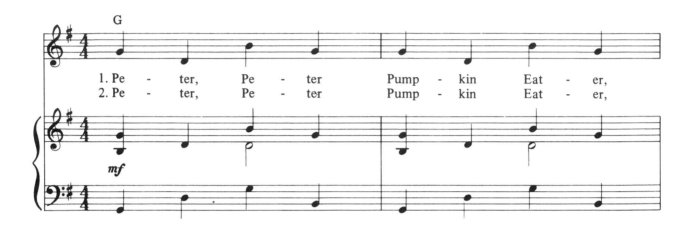

1. Pe - ter, Pe - ter Pump - kin Eat - er,
2. Pe - ter, Pe - ter Pump - kin Eat - er,

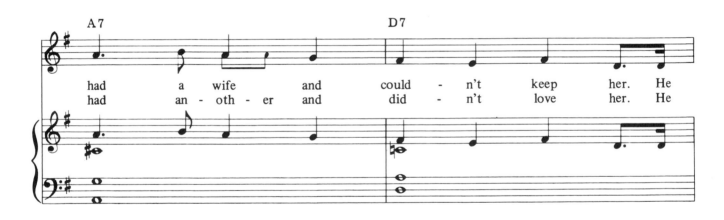

had a wife and could - n't keep her. He
had an - oth - er and did - n't love her. He

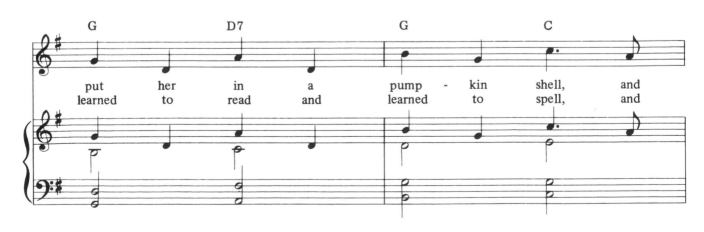

put her in a pump - kin shell, and
learned to read and learned to spell, and

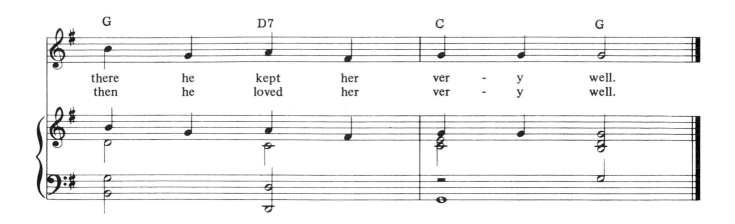

there   he   kept   her   ver - y   well.
then   he   loved   her   ver - y   well.

POLLY PUT THE KETTLE ON

1. Pol - ly put the ket - tle on, Pol - ly put the ket - tle on,
2. Now put down the gin - ger cake, now put down the gin - ger cake,

Pol - ly put the ket - tle on, we'll all have tea.
Now put down the gin - ger cake, we'll all take tea.

Suk - ey take it off a - gain, Suk - ey take it off a - gain,
Stir the fire and let it bake, stir the fire and let it bake,

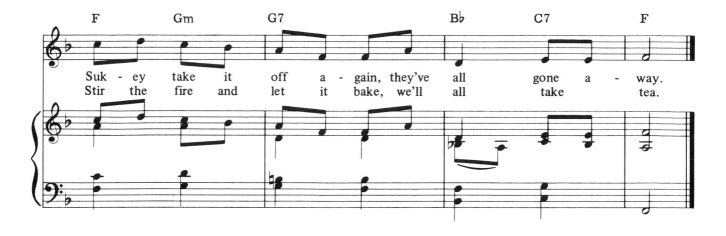

Suk - ey take it off a - gain, they've all gone a - way.
Stir the fire and let it bake, we'll all take tea.

3. Polly set the table out, *(three times)*
   We'll all take tea.
   Move the dishes all about, *(three times)*
   We'll all take tea.

4. Pass around the punkin pie, *(three times)*
   We'll all take tea.
   And the fritters made of rye, *(three times)*
   We'll all take tea.

POP GOES THE WEASEL

All a-round the cob-bler's bench, the mon-key chased the wea - sel, the mon-key thought 'twas all___ in fun, Pop! goes the wea - sel. A pen - ny for a spool___ of thread, a pen - ny for a nee - dle,

That's the way the mon - ey goes, pop! goes the wea - sel.

RIDE A COCKHORSE

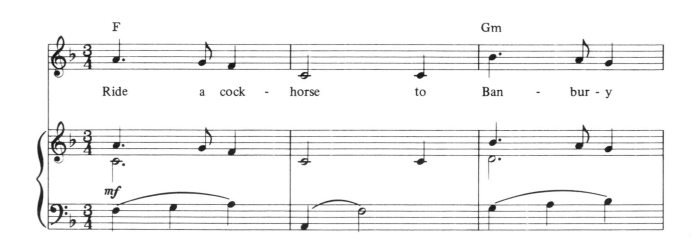

Ride a cock - horse to Ban - bur - y

Cross, to see a fine la - dy up-

ROCK-A-BYE BABY

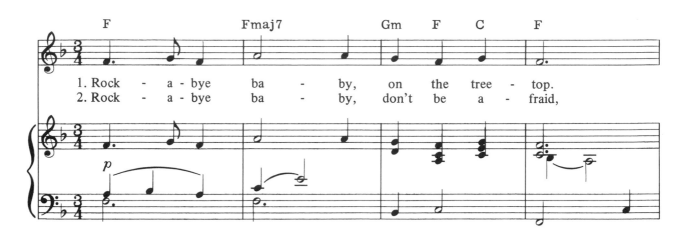

1. Rock - a-bye ba - by, on the tree - top.
2. Rock - a-bye ba - by, don't be a - fraid,

When the wind blows, the cra - dle will rock.
It was a dream, a trick your will mind played.

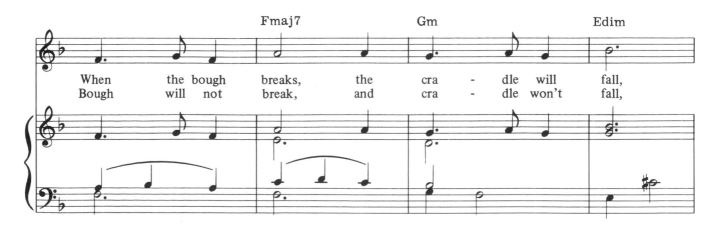

When the bough breaks, the cra - dle will fall,
Bough will not break, and cra - dle won't fall,

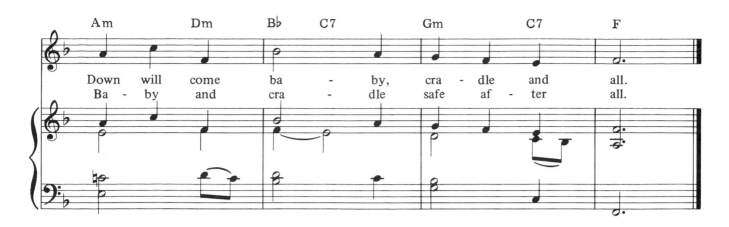

Down will come ba — by, cra — dle and all.
Ba — by and cra — dle safe af — ter all.

SEE-SAW, MARJORIE DAW

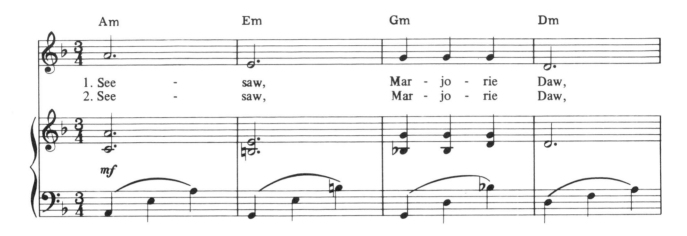

1. See - saw, Mar - jo - rie Daw,
2. See - saw, Mar - jo - rie Daw,

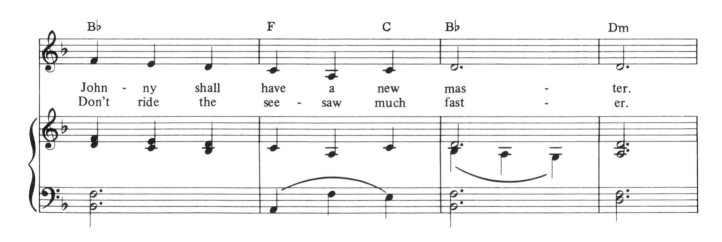

John - ny shall have a new mas - ter.
Don't ride the see - saw much fast - er.

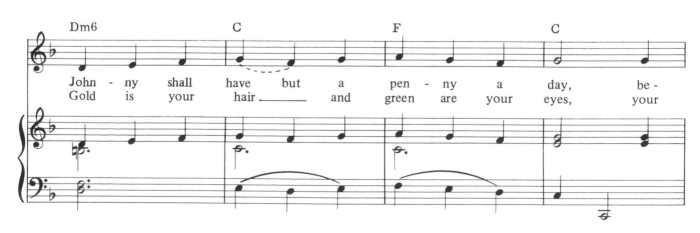

John - ny shall have but a pen - ny a day, be -
Gold is your hair ___ and green are your eyes, your

70

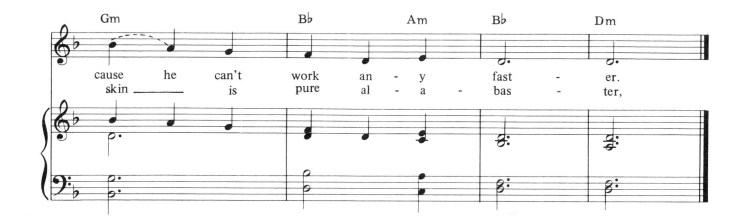

cause   he   can't   work   an   -   y   fast   -   er.
skin _____ is   pure   al   -   a   -   bas   -   ter,

Simple Simon

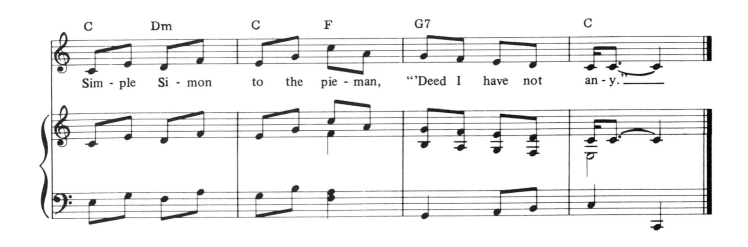

Sim - ple Si - mon to the pie - man, "'Deed I have not an - y."

SING A SONG OF SIXPENCE

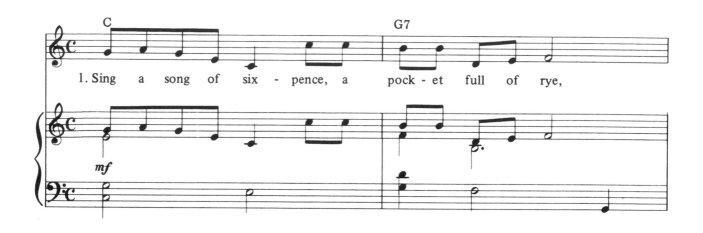

1. Sing a song of six - pence, a pock - et full of rye,

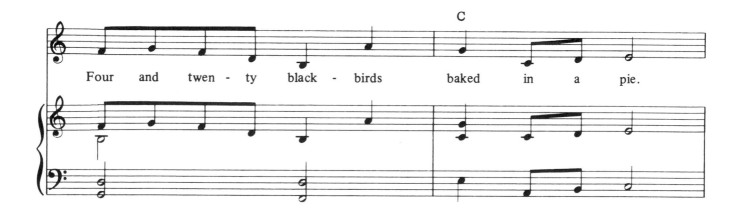

Four and twen - ty black - birds baked in a pie.

When the pie was o - pened the birds be - gan to sing,

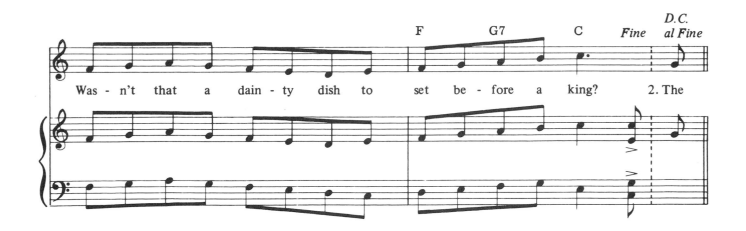

Was - n't that a dain - ty dish to set be - fore a king? 2. The

2. The king was in his counting house,
counting out his money.
The queen was in the parlor,
eating bread and honey.
The maid was in the garden
hanging out the clothes.
Along came a blackbird
and snipped off her nose.

TAFFY

1. Taf - fy was a Welsh - man, Taf - fy was a thief.
2. Taf - fy was a Welsh - man, Taf - fy was a thief.

Taf - fy came to my house and stole a leg of beef.
Taf - fy came to my house and stole a leg of beef.

I went to Taf - fy's house, Taf - fy was - n't home,
I went to Taf - fy's house, Taf - fy was in bed, I

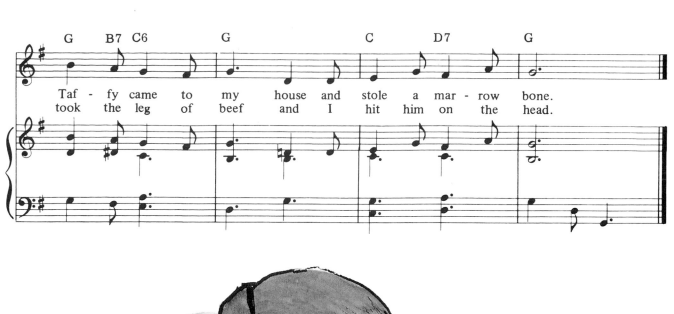

Taf - fy came to my house and stole a mar - row bone.
took the leg of my beef and I hit him on the head.

THERE WAS A CROOKED MAN

There was a crook-ed man, and he walked a crook-ed mile, he found a crook-ed six-pence be-side a crook-ed stile. He bought a crook-ed cat who ___ caught a crook-ed mouse, and they

There Was a Little Girl

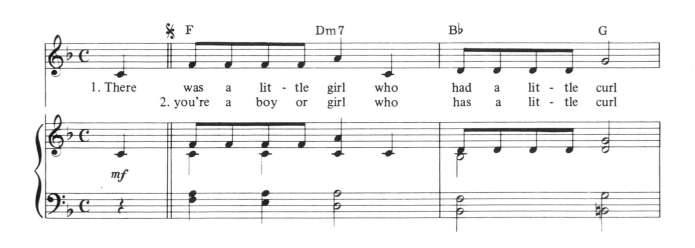

1. There was a lit-tle girl who had a lit-tle curl
2. you're a boy or girl who has a lit-tle curl

right in the mid-dle of her fore-head, —— and
right in the mid-dle of your fore-head, —— I

when she was good, she was ver - y, ver - y good, but
hope you are good, but if some - times you are bad, I

when she was bad she was hor - rid. _____ This
hope you will nev - er be hor - rid. _____

pret - ty lit - tle girl, with a pret - ty lit - tle curl,

right in the mid - dle of her fore - head, _____ was

THERE WAS AN OLD WOMAN

There was an old wom - an who lived in a shoe, she

had so man - y chil - dren that she did - n't know what to do. She

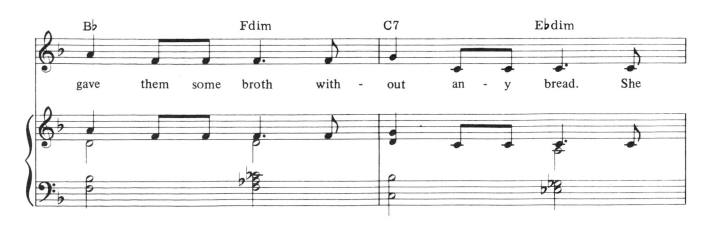

gave them some broth with - out an - y bread. She

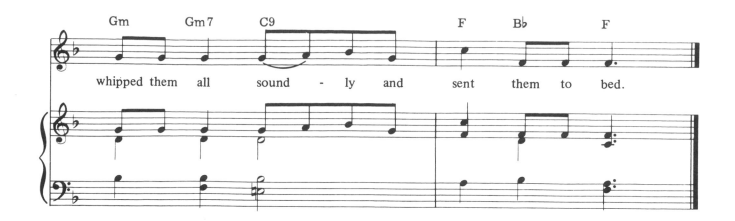

whipped them all sound - ly and sent them to bed.

THIS LITTLE PIG

This lit - tle pig went to mar - ket, this lit - tle pig stayed home; this lit - tle pig had roast beef, this lit - tle pig had none; and this lit - tle pig cried,

THREE BLIND MICE

THREE LITTLE KITTENS

1. Three lit-tle kit-tens, they lost their mit-tens and they be-gan to cry, "Oh,
2. Three lit-tle kit-tens, they found their mit-tens and they be-gan to cry, "Oh,

Moth-er, dear, we sad-ly fear, our mit-tens we have lost." "What!
Moth-er, dear, see here, see here, our mit-tens we have found." "What!

Lost your mit-tens, you naught-y kit-tens, then you shall have no pie."
Found your mit-tens, you dar-ling kit-tens, then you shall have some pie."

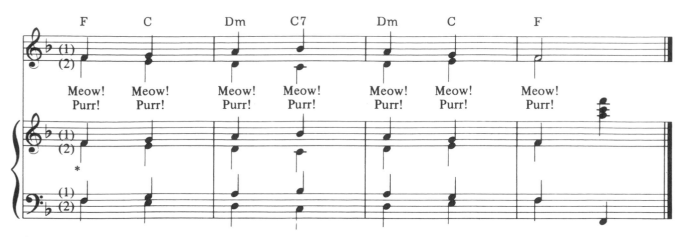

Meow! Purr! Meow! Purr! Meow! Purr! Meow! Purr! Meow! Purr! Meow! Purr! Meow! Purr!

*Play (1) and (2) separately in unison, single lines only (bass and treble, not in harmony).

3. The three little kittens put on their mittens
   And soon ate up the pie.
   "Oh, mother, dear, we greatly fear,
   Our mittens we have soiled."
   "What! Soiled your mittens, you naughty kittens."
   Then they began to sigh.
   Meow! Meow! *etc. (first tune)*

4. The three little kittens, they washed their mittens
   And hung them up to dry.
   "Oh, mother, dear, look here, look here,
   Our mittens we have washed."   *SPOKEN:*
   "What! Washed you mittens, you darling kittens – (but hush!)
   I smell a rat close by!"
   Meow! Meow! *etc. (first tune)*

TO MARKET

To mar - ket, to mar - ket, to buy a fat pig,

Home a - gain, home a - gain, jig - get - y jig. To

mar - ket, to mar - ket, to buy a fat hog,

TOM, TOM, THE PIPER'S SON

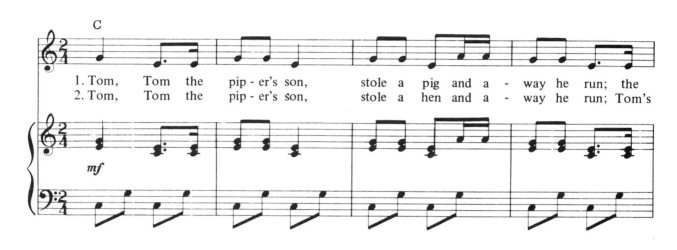

1. Tom, Tom the pip - er's son, stole a pig and a - way he run; the
2. Tom, Tom the pip - er's son, stole a hen and a - way he run; Tom's

pig was eat and Tom was beat, and Tom ran cry - ing down the street.
out of luck, the hen said "Cluck," and drove a - way in a pick - up truck.

3. Tom, Tom the piper's son,
   Stole a duck and away he run;
   the duck said, "Quack,"
   Tom gave it back,
   His mother gave him a right sharp smack.

4. Tom, Tom the piper's son,
   Stole a ghost and away he run;
   the ghost said, "Boo!"
   And Tom said, "Ooh!"
   And the ghost disappeared up the chimney flue.